2·50

PORTRAITS OF JESUS

Mark

A4 4

PORTRAITS OF JESUS

Mark

A CONTEXTUAL APPROACH
to Bible Study

by
Michele Guttler

COLLINS

Collins Liturgical Publications
8 Grafton Street, London W1X 3LA

Collins Liturgical in USA
Icehouse One — 401
151 Union Street, San Francisco, CA 94111-1299

Collins Liturgical in Canada
Novalis, Box 9700, Terminal
375 Rideau St, Ottawa, Ontario K1G 4B4

Distributed in Ireland by
Educational Company of Ireland
21 Talbot Street, Dublin 1

Collins Liturgical Australia
PO Box 316, Blackburn, Victoria 3130

Collins Liturgical New Zealand
PO Box 1, Auckland

ISBN 0 00 599973 1
© 1987 text Michele Guttler, illustrations Wm Collins
First published 1987

Cover illustration by Velile Soha
Cover design by Malcolm Harvey Young
Typographical design by Colin Reed
Typeset by John Swain & Son Limited
Made and printed in Great Britain
by Collins, Glasgow

Library of Congress Cataloging-in-Publication Data

Guttler, Michele.
    Portraits of Jesus: Mark.

    Bibliography: p.
    1. Jesus Christ — History of doctrines — Early church, ca. 30-600.
    2. Bible. N.T. Mark — Criticism, interpretation, etc.
    3. Bible. N.T. Mark — Study.   I. Bible. N.T. Mark.   II. Title.
BT198.G87 1988   226'.306   87-18298
ISBN 0-00-599973-1 (pbk.)

Contents

General Introduction

This study is part of a series of commentaries on the four gospels. The aim of the series is to present the distinct portrait of Jesus which each gospel provides, and yet to do so in a way which shows how the four portraits relate to and complement each other. None of the volumes is therefore intended to be a comprehensive commentary on a particular gospel. The passages chosen for study and reflection have been selected because they portray most vividly the portrait which the evangelist wishes to paint. Yet, when all four volumes are taken as a whole, it will be seen that they cover a great deal of the material found in the four gospels.

The origin of the series is important for understanding what has been attempted. Each of the four authors is a biblical scholar well versed in the contemporary discussion on the gospels. In particular, each has a special interest in the sociology of the New Testament and a contextual approach to Christian faith and theology. Even though much scholarly work lies behind each volume, the authors have not sought to engage in scholarly debate. They have provided, rather, commentaries for use in Bible study groups and by people at the 'grass-roots'. Indeed, the commentaries originated as much within such groups as they did within the scholar's study. For several months each author met with various Bible study groups comprised of people from different denominational, racial and socio-economic backgrounds. Together they explored the gospels in order to discern who Jesus really is for us today. Hence the attempt to locate the portrait of Jesus in three contexts or horizons: his own context; the context of the original evangelist and those to whom the gospel was written; and our own situation today. Each of these is pertinent to understanding who Jesus is for us, and they also provide a way into the study of the gospels which has already proved useful in Bible study groups.

The authors have worked as a team, and each of the four volumes follow a similar pattern. All have used the New International Version of the Bible, and, as already indicated, a premium has been placed by all on a sociological approach to the text. Each volume also contains suggestions as to how they can best be used. There is, therefore, a basic structure common to all four volumes. Yet each author has brought to the task different insights and experiences, gained, not least, from discussing the gospels with people who are struggling in different contexts to be faithful to Jesus Christ in South Africa. This, rather than some rigid formula, has shaped the final product. It is our hope that other Bible study groups will find them of value and use for their own journey of faith and obedience within their particular historical and social context. Our overriding concern is that each person discover the Jesus to whom the four evangelists bear witness.

John W. de Gruchy
Bill Domeris
General Editors

This work developed during times of great turbulence and sadness in South Africa.
May truth, understanding and a true quest for justice arise from reflecting on the message of the bible as it speaks to people in troubled situations everywhere.

Introduction: Framing the Portrait

Three Horizons

Mark's gospel is similar to the other gospels in that they all tell the story of Jesus; they tell about his life, teachings, travels, about his death and resurrection. Apart from sharing these common points, each gospel is specific and unique. To understand Mark's gospel properly, we need to discover what Mark's unique features are, and then try to decide why Mark used these special tools in writing his version of the story of Jesus.

Whenever people write, whether it be a newspaper editorial, a commentary on a sports match or a novel, they have to know their subject material well and they need to know who their audience is, and what that audience wants to read. Mark's subject material was Jesus and Jesus' life and activities in Palestine. His audience was the Roman Christians. To these two 'horizons' to the portrait of Jesus which Mark painted, the reader needs to add a third horizon. We need to recognise our own context, as our position in the world and the type of society which we come from will shape the way we read and understand the message in Mark's gospel.

Before turning to read and study Mark's gospel we will first take a close look at each of these three horizons. Equipped with this insight, Mark's gospel can be read and understood in a new meaningful way.

The first horizon: Palestine

The setting for the story of Jesus is Palestine, and much of the material in the gospels deals with Jesus' activities in, and travels around Palestine. To understand Jesus' actions, and to come to terms with the problems and issues facing this multi-faceted community, we need to begin by examining the various aspects which make up the essence of early Palestine. In other words we need to examine the context in which Jesus lived and worked, so that when we read about tenant farmers, stewards or scribes, we immediately know who they are, and where they fitted into Palestinian society.

The best way truly to get 'into' the community and really begin to understand that society, will be through looking at Palestine in different aspects. Through examining the economic life of Palestine, one gets a thorough picture of the social classes and political framework governing the area.

Palestine's Economy

Galilee and Judea were two separate provinces, both annexed to the Roman empire. This annexation meant that they were forced into the economic structure of the empire. This new economic system, in which they had to participate, forced a rapid destruction of the accepted values, customs and norms in both areas. We shall examine the economic activities in two main spheres, namely, that which occurs on the land and the economy of the towns. In each of these two different spheres we will clearly be able to see how the people were alienated, and cut off from their traditional lifestyles. With the change in the economy brought about by Roman occupation, many changes in other areas were triggered off.

Rural Areas

Most of the farming took place in Galilee as it was more fertile than the relatively arid Judea. The economic life in Galilee was beginning to undergo a series of important changes. Before Roman occupation, land was owned by the people who farmed it, and was farmed in a subsistence manner or the produce used for bartering. Subsistence farming means that the farmer produces enough for his family's needs, and that any remaining crops are used to barter with. A good example would be that of a farmer who on producing more olives than his family needs, might swop some olives with another farmer for a bushel of wheat. Before Roman occupation, produce was not sold on a market: farming occurred on land owned by the peasant farmer, who thus had a vested interest in the condition of the land, as well as the amount produced from his land.

With the advent of Roman occupation, another form of land ownership was introduced. This was the system of *latifundia*, or large farming concerns. These large farms were worked by landless peasants, who obviously had no real interest in the quality or quantity of crops produced. These *latifundia* were created on royal land, which was either land that had been confiscated, or land which had been won in battle. The system of *latifundia* allowed unrest to ferment. The peasants who had previously worked the land which they owned felt as if their birthright was being denied them. Their relationship with Yahweh — the Lord — rested to a large degree on the notion that Palestine was the promised land, given to the Jews to own, and that the Romans were defiling their covenant relationship with Yahweh. All land ownership was the privilege of the empire, and the Jews were merely allowed to administer it.

Within the rural sphere, under Roman rule, there were three basic economic groups, namely, the free peasant, the tenant farmer and the large-scale landowner. Each of these three groups needs to be examined in more detail.

1 *The Free Peasant*   The free peasants owned the land which they farmed, which meant that they had a special interest in the condition of the land and in the quality and quantity of crops produced. They were taxed fiscally (i.e. in cash) only. This form of taxation meant that they needed to sell their produce, in order to raise the cash necessary for their taxes. In order to have sufficient produce to sell as well as to live off, their methods of farming and of production had to change and improve. Production also needed to become more effecient because they were now competing on a limited market with the *latifundia*.

The fishermen on the Sea of Galilee belong to this class too: although they did not own their own particular 'patch' of sea, they worked for themselves as opposed to a landowner. These fishermen often teamed up with others to make their fishing more productive. Great nets, 500m in length, requiring several boats and six to eight fishermen to handle, became a common sight upon the Sea of Galilee. Luke 5.7 shows us a gospel record of the collaboration between the fishermen. The main reason for the collaboration between the fishermen is that they were also taxed fiscally and so needed to catch and sell more fish to meet their tax demands and still feed their families.

2 *The Tenant Farmer*   Tenant farmers found employment on the *latifundia*. They were displaced peasants who had lost the ownership rights on their land (usually as a result of tax defaults). These people now found employment as hired labour, and it is this group who feature in the stories of Lk.16.1-6 and Mk 12.1-9. These tenant farmers

had to bear the brunt of an excesssively heavy tax burden, they were taxed both in kind (which means that a percentage of their produce was to be given to the Romans) as well as being taxed fiscally. The standard wage for hired daily labour was one silver denarius, which was completely inadequate for a family to subsist on. Poor wages, as well as a lack of work (for there were many of these dispossessed people living in Galilee) served as a stimulus to encourage the people to move to the towns.

3 *The Large Scale Landowner* This was the wealthy class, and comprised of people who were well placed within the ruling circles. This group had bought up much of the land when the free peasants defaulted on their tax or had to move into the rural areas to meet financial demands. They tended to live in the developing towns or in Jerusalem and can thus be described as absentee landlords. As a result of not living on their farms, they had to hire stewards to control their affairs and manage their estates. The stewards also controlled and paid the daily hired labour, but this system was open to corruption, as is shown in the parable of Lk.16.1-13. Naturally, this wealthy class was viewed critically by the poorer classes, and were often perceived to be greedy, self-centered and hard. Lk.12.16-21 is an effective representation of the poorer classes' image of the landowning classes. They were perceived as a group who were becoming increasingly decadent.

On the privately owned lands as well as on the *latifundia*, grain was produced (crops of corn and also pulse). The farms also cultivated cereals, fruit and vegetables (eg: olives, figs, grapes and even chick peas.) Wheel-less ploughs and scythes were used to cultivate the land. To some degree, livestock was kept on the *latifundia*, although these farms were mainly concerned with large-scale crop production. A market for cattle, chickens and doves was to be found within the confines of the temple, as they were offered as sacrifices.

Sheep and goats were raised in the arid areas of Judea, and the larger livestock was raised on the coastal plains. Pigs, being unclean animals, were not raised in Palestine, and Mk 5.1-20 must be seen as occurring in a foreign country.

Urban Areas
The second sphere of economic life which we need to examine is that

of the urban economy. During the period that Jesus lived and worked in Palestine as well as during the time that the gospels were penned, towns were developing and growing. This occurred because as the peasants found it increasingly difficult to meet the demands of taxation and still make a reasonable living, they began to move from their farms into the urban areas where they would seek employment. Many Jews joined the Roman army as a means to avoid starvation.

The developing towns were completely dependant for food on the rural areas. While there certainly was a class of artisans, the middle class which has since become so synonymous with towns was notably small or absent. This serves as a sharp contrast to the situation which we find during the period described in the book of Acts.

The typical form of industry during the period was that of the craftsman, where the final product was sold directly to the consumer without a middle person. Both Jesus and Paul originally belonged to this class, Jesus as a carpenter and Paul as a tentmaker (Acts 22.3; 18.3). The main items manufactured in the towns, or more specifically, in Jerusalem were sold by weavers, leather merchants and carpenters. Gold and silver smiths and seal makers were also common professions and luxury items such as resins, ointments and jewellery were also produced in Jerusalem. These artisans were usually self-employed.

There was much building activity in Jerusalem. The construction of the Temple served as a source of employment for many citizens for the duration of the 80 years of construction (begun in 20 BCE, the Temple was only completed in 64 CE*). More than 18,000 workmen were employed in the construction of the Temple. Skilled artisans, such as carpenters and stone masons, were engaged in the building project. After construction was completed, a large number of people were employed to maintain the Temple. The Temple also offered employment to numerous teachers of the law, people of the treasury and people selling sacrifices. The Temple thus served as a great economic boon to the city.

As well as the economic groups which have already been examined, the society of Palestine was made up of employees of the Roman empire and those who worked for the Jewish authorities.

---

* BCE = Before Christian Era (i.e. BC); CE = Christian Era (i.e. AD).

Political Formation in Palestine

From 6CE, the area was ruled by the Romans. The Roman 'chief' of the area was a *Prefect* or Procurator. From 25CE to 35CE, the Roman Prefect was Pontius Pilatus, who was involved in Jesus' trial. He headed the Roman officials and the garrison stationed in the area. The Prefect, although directly responsible to Rome for the conditions in Palestine, left daily legislation to the Jews themselves.

The legislative procedure was in the hands of the 72 member *Sanhedrin*, most of whom were Sadducees by birth. They met under the leadership of the High Priest, who belonged to the ruling aristocracy of Rome. The High Priest during Jesus' time was Caiaphas, but the former High Priest, Annas, continued to wield much control. Five families belonging to the ruling aristocracy controlled Judea through the High Priest. These five families controlled the Temple, its finances and generally the religious life of the people.

The Temple of Jerusalem was the focal point of the country. People gathered there for festivals throughout the year. The Temple was more than a religious institution however. It exercised tax demands on the people, and served as a source of employment for many residents of Jerusalem. Moneychangers made much profit working within the confines of the temple. Coins from all over the Roman empire were exchanged, with the moneychangers making a profit on each deal. Coins were exchanged for Temple shekels necessary for Temple tax and to buy sacrifices. The Temple also taxed all Jews in Palestine in order to assist with building operations. These taxes were extremely high and the lower clergy often saw very little of the funds.

Exploitation by the Temple and the Sadducees, and the Roman occupation made life for those living in Galilee and Palestine extremely difficult. This difficult time and the problems experienced by the people were directly addressed by Jesus in his teachings and works.

Social Groups in Palestine

Many of the social groups distinctive to Palestine have been described in the preceding section. The religious groupings have not yet been mentioned however. Often in Mark's gospel one reads of the scribes, pharisees or Sadducees, without knowing the difference between these groups or what they stand for. To understand why these groups were antagonistic toward Jesus, or why Jesus entered into debate with them, we need first to examine the groups.

Scribes   The scribes were a heterogeneous group, comprised of people from the priestly aristocracy as well as the lower clergy. They were extremely well trained, and their 'power' and authority lay in their knowledge. As teachers, they exercised great influence on the people. They were given responsible positions within the Sanhedrin and Pharisaic groups, and because they were trained in the law, they exerted much influence in these groups.

Most of the scribes lived in real poverty, and they were financially assisted by their students and by alms given to them by the Temple. Jesus was compared to the scribes (Mk 1.22), showing that he too had much knowledge. Jesus' main criticism of the scribes was that although they had learned much, they were unable to communicate their knowledge to the people, their words were incomprehensible to the Jews (Lk.11.52). They were also criticised for trying to emulate the pharisees.

Pharisees   The pharisees were united by a desire to maintain fidelity and commitment to the requirements of the law. There were roughly 6,000 pharisees during the time of Herod. This number was made up of people belonging to all social 'classes', although the majority were small merchants, artisans and peasants and on the whole, poorly educated. Many Levites (priests of lower rank) also became pharisees.

The pharisees encouraged 'separatism', and developed a sense of superiority toward people who did not meet the requirements of the Jewish faith, either through 'fault of birth' or deed. Jesus was extremely critical toward the self-righteous attitude of the pharisees (Lk.18.9-14). There was some animosity between the pharisees and the priests, whom the pharisees felt should not presume holiness merely because of their position in the synagogues: to the pharisees, holiness was the result of obedience alone. Pharisees were often arbitrators between the authorities and the people, because of their strict observance of the law.

Mk 2.23 - 28 shows the different way that Jesus and the Pharisees interpreted the law. Jesus examines the law in the relevant context, and criticises the pharisees for their blind following of the law. The pharisees are completely bound by the law: Jesus examines the law in terms of the community and revitalises it.

Sadducees   Not much is known about the Sadducees. They were characterised by an extremely conservative interpretation of the law. Their numbers were made up primarily from members of the ruling class. They were zealous defenders of the status quo and interpreted the law literally. They saw their dominant wealthy positions in society as a sign of divine approval. This interpretation of the law shows how the ruling class may profit by developing one strand of religious interpretation in favour of others, thus justifying their position to the rest of society.

Jesus was probably referring to this class when he uttered his curse on the rich (Lk.6.24). The synoptic gospels make it clear that it was members of this class who were responsible for the condemnation of Jesus. Their animosity can be understood, as Jesus certainly spoke out against the rich and in favour of the poor: clearly this was perceived as a threat to their existence.

The second horizon: Rome

Biblical scholars seem quite sure that the gospel of Mark was written to the Christians living in Rome around 70 AD, just following the death of the emperor Nero. We can never be totally sure that this was Mark's audience because the gospels, unlike the New Testament letters, do not say who they are addressing. Evidence seems to suggest however that the Roman Christians were the first recipients of Mark's gospel. To understand the gospel, it would be helpful to examine the likely audience. We need to turn to the Rome of 2000 years ago, and carefully examine the society, the economy and the political conditions, all of which would have influenced Mark's audience in Rome.

All scholars today agree that Mark's gospel was written by a man, although his exact identity is hidden from us. Throughout this text we will be using the masculine pronouns when discussing the author of this gospel, although we recognise that future new evidence might prove this accepted notion wrong.

A Christian living in Rome during this time certainly had good reason to feel nervous. Jerusalem had been destroyed by Titus in the previous year (70 AD) following the Jewish revolt, and Rome itself was in a state of political upheaval as a result of the death of Nero in 68 AD. Civil war was waged on all fronts, between possible candidates for emperor. Finally in 69 AD Vespasian succeeded and became emperor.

Although the Roman Empire was experiencing problems politically, the Empire was still at its peak and was very strong. Geographically, it had expanded to its limits, and many territories far from Rome had been conquered and were now under Roman rule. With the conquering of many lands, lifestyles changed dramatically, not only for the people living in the newly conquered lands but for the citizens of Rome and Italy as well. Changes were experienced economically, politically and socially. These three areas will be examined more fully, in an attempt to identify with the problems which faced the Christians living in Rome.

Economic Position

The city of Rome was becoming a financial drain on the rest of the empire. The conquered lands were taxed extensively, and these taxes as well as loot from pillaging all made their way to Rome. This situation suited the Roman governors and merchants, and their wealth began increasing dramatically. Small business-men and farmers, however, were forced out of work as there was no longer a market for their produce, as a result of a massive programme of importation which had begun.

Farmers lost their livelihood: take, for example, an Italian wine farmer. Previously, his wine and grapes could be sold with little competition on the market in Rome; now however, superior wine was imported from the conquered area of Gaul, and with this added competition, many farmers could no longer survive.

The Roman economy rested on slave labour. The slaves were considered the property of their owner. During the reign of Vespasian, the total slave population living in Rome has been estimated at about half a million. Most of the slaves worked on the large farming estates, *latifundia*. These *latifundia* were created when the wealthier farmers bought up the land from the surrounding farmers who had gone bankrupt and moved to Rome. Slave labour was used because after the initial outlay of buying the slaves, they cost the farmer little in upkeep. The children of the slaves were considered as the property of the slave owners, and could thus be sold, which also increased their profit. Freemen on the other hand obviously demanded a salary and could be conscripted to the Roman army, so the use of slaves grew and the slave population increased dramatically.

This dependence on slave labour caused a rapid depopulation of the countryside with the new landless people moving into Rome where they would often be unemployed. Rome became overpopulated, with filthy, unhygienic slums spreading throughout the city. Squalid conditions were only one side of the coin however. Opulent, luxurious homes served as a sharp contrast to the depravation all around. The city of Rome was now completely dependent on the slaves and the provinces for survival, and the population of Rome naturally harboured feelings of resentment toward the emperor because of the hardships to which they were being subjected.

Political Situation

The Roman Empire was a military dictatorship, ruled by the emperor who was also the commander-in-chief of the army. He possessed all the power which had previously been shared between the senate (which represented the landowning families) and the people, representing the citizens of Rome.

Although Rome was ruled by the emperor, the system was not very stable, with civil wars continually raging between possible contenders to the position of emperor.

In order to ensure that he remain in power, it was essential for the emperor to have the support of the new imperial bureaucracy, which he was helping to constitute from freed imperial slaves. His new bureaucracy gradually began to take power away from the senators. The emperor needed support from outside of the senatorial class (his traditional source of support), because it was from their ranks that competition to his power arose.

Another threat to the rule of the emperor came from the military leaders. Within the bounds of the empire, provincial uprisings and military mutinies, such as the rebellion of the Zealots in Palestine, were common.

There are numerous accounts of the outrageous behaviour of the Roman emperors such as Nero who perceived the Christians to be a threat. The Roman historian, Tacitus, records how Nero held the Christians to be responsible for the fire of 64CE. Tacitus tells of how Nero himself assisted in the many tortures inflicted upon those accused of being Christians.

Religion and Values

The ruling senatorial nobility were naturally affected by their immense wealth, and now because they were becoming deprived of their earlier power, they began to drift into a life of drunkenness and debauchery.

The old Roman religion with its concept of a pantheon of gods was becoming increasingly corrupt and 'diluted', resulting in 'new' religions from the East increasing in popularity and acceptance amongst the citizens of Rome. These religions found much support and sympathy amongst the landless peasants, the unemployed and the freed slaves. One of these new religions was Christianity.

The Christian Community

In the midst of this world of poverty and deprivation as well as opulence and wealth, we find the Christian community. It is perhaps false to call the christians a community because the evidence we have shows that they were a cosmopolitan group, coming from all walks and stations of life, and that their number was not confined to any specific economic or social class alone.

It seems likely that there were Jews living in Rome from the second century BCE, but that they only began to immigrate in any large numbers in the following century. The Jewish community itself was not homogeneous, and while a number of Jews pursued lucrative mercantile careers, the majority seem to have subsisted at a lower economic level. There was more than one synagogue in Rome, unlike many cities of the ancient world, and this fact added to the diversity amongst its Jewish citizens. The Christian message would thus have been received differently by the existing Jewish communities of the different synagogues.

It is not certain when the Christian message reached Rome, or how long Christianity had been practised there, but in 49 AD a group, thought to be Christians, were expelled from Rome (see Acts 18.2). Romans 1.7 tells us that Paul wrote his letter to the Christians in Rome in 58 AD; and in 64 AD the emporer Nero blamed the Christians for the fire which razed Rome.

Like the Jewish community, the Christian 'church' seems to have been a motley group of people. The names mentioned in Romans 16 show us that the community was made up of Romans, Greeks, Jews, slaves and freedmen. Other biblical references attesting the existence of a Christian community in Rome can be found in Col.4.10ff; 2 Tim.4.21 and Acts 28.15. All that these references really tell us is that at the time of the emperor Vespasian, there was a relatively large, diverse group of Christians living in Rome.

This group of Christians was probably mostly made up from the lower social classes, and the majority do not seem to be Jewish (see Romans 11.13). The Christian church at Rome was led by *presbyters* (church elders), yet the Christians did not have any official places to use for gatherings and tended instead to meet in peoples' homes. The Christian community gathered for meals, prayer and worship, and to read collected stories of Jesus and the letters from the apostles.

The early Christians were continually expecting the return of Jesus, and the gospel of Mark, written after Paul's letter to the Romans, bears witness to the disappointment that their hope for deliverance had not yet beeen fulfilled. Mark's gospel also speaks directly to the suffering experienced by the Roman Christians. Emphases such as the centrality of the cross (chapters 14-15) and the necessity for suffering and serving within discipleship (8.34-8; 10.38-45 and 13.9-13) both show Mark's concern in writing to a community experiencing harsh persecution.

This picture of Rome, the second horizon, will help us to understand the various concerns and emphases which come through in Mark's gospel.

The third horizon: our own context

Just as one needs to understand the world in which Jesus lived, and the community to which Mark wrote, it is important to recognise our own position within the world and more specifically, our community.

This book is being written in South Africa. South Africa is a country of tension, oppression and anger. The wider Christian community comprises people of all races and socio-economic groups. Mark's gospel speaks directly to Christians living within this troubled situation.

One might question how a document written two thousand years ago could still be relevant today, or could still address today's issues. The facade of political pressures, economic exploitation or social injustice may have altered, but the issues remain basically the same.

Mark had experienced these hardships first-hand, as had his audience. Mark witnesses to Jesus' response within these various situations. Christians in South Africa and in other parts of the world need to ask how Jesus would respond if placed within their context, and be obedient to his example.

As I am the writer of this work, my own horizon is important to recognise. I live in a white, 'middle-class' suburb in Cape Town; a suburb which is surrounded by townships (black residential areas) and 'coloured' suburbs. The Group Areas Act forces people of different races to live in different prescribed areas. The biblical texts used in this book were discussed with people living in these different areas. It was really interesting having the different interpretations on the texts from these various groups, as the experiences of people were clearly reflected in the way that they understood the message behind the texts.

It is unnecessary to describe the conditions in South Africa further. It is a land which is both beautiful and full of promise as well as being a country enforcing discrimination and racial tension, often in the name of Christianity.

The people contributing to the studies in this book are located in all of the racial and socio-economic groups making up this country. Some might be regarded as privileged, others as deprived. The common thread uniting this multi-faceted group is a sincere desire to obey Jesus, and to respond to situations in the way in which Jesus' authority commands them.

Mark's Portrait of Jesus

Jesus, God's Secret Agent

The gospel of Mark is the shortest of the synoptic gospels (Matthew, Mark and Luke). Each of the gospels has a specific picture or portrait of Jesus which emerges through the recounting of the teachings, miracles and life of Jesus. What are the characteristics of Mark's portrait of Jesus?

The Style of Mark

Characteristic of Mark's style is the simple manner in which he wrote. The gospel was written in Greek, the second official language of the Roman Empire. Mark's Greek was grammatically weak, structurally clumsy and used a limited vocabulary, suggesting that this was not his home language. His use of Semitic expressions which he immediately translates for his readers (eg. 3.17; 5.41; 7.11; 7.34; 14.36 and 15.16) suggests that he was a Jewish writer, but that his audience was ignorant of the meanings of the expressions. Marks' style of writing includes many Roman words and phrases such as centurion 15.39; legion 5.9; praetorium 15.16 and cohort 15.16 amongst others. Thus on the whole the stylistic features of Mark's gospel suggest a Jewish writer who had difficulty expressing himself in Greek, writing to a Roman audience.

The Identity of Mark

Mark's gospel is written in a simple and 'rough' way, with a vigorous style. This style, together with its special descriptions and details suggest that the gospel is written by an eye-witness. Is this the case? Witnesses (such as Bishop Papias) in the second and third centuries first attributed this gospel to Mark, but it is uncertain exactly who this Mark was.

Acts speaks of one 'John surnamed Mark' (12.12), whose mother's house served as a refuge for Peter after he was released from prison. This same Mark was taken by Barnabas, his cousin (Col.4.10), and by Paul (Acts 12.25) to Antioch. He also accompanied Barnabas to

Cyprus (Acts 15.37-39). This may be the same Mark who Paul says is in Rome (Col.4.10; 2 Tim.4.11). Peter also makes reference to a Mark (1 Peter 5.13), but we can never be absolutely sure if this is the same author of the gospel.

The gospel might be a *pseudepigraphy*, which is a text attributed to a famous person in order to lend authority to the text. This is the case with other biblical books. Many scholars today feel that John Mark, the disciple of Peter, was the gospel's author because of the numerous instances of a seemingly 'eye-witness' account of Jesus' activities, which the author might have been told by Peter.

Special Features of Mark's Gospel

Mark gives us a human picture of Jesus
Mark goes to great lengths to show his readers Jesus' human qualities and attributes. Mark tells us that Jesus slept when he was tired (4.38); that he felt hungry (11.12); that when confronted with suffering he was moved with compassion (1.41) and that Jesus experienced both anger and indignation (3.5; 10.14). Mark shows his readers that they can identify fully with Jesus because he experienced many of the things which they are going through. Mark shows us how Jesus was fully human, sharing in the joy and sadness of the human experience.

Mark writes in vivid detail
Mark shows how Jesus slept with his head on a pillow during the storm (4.38). He describes the feeding of the multitude in great detail, going so far as to stress the greenness of the grass (6.39f). He shows how Jesus held the children in his arms (10.16). A striking picture which Mark draws for his readers is that of the lonely figure of Jesus walking ahead of his disciples on his way to Jerusalem. These characteristics of the gospel show that an eye witness had recounted these stories which were later recorded by Mark.

Mark's account is simple and direct
Mark's gospel is short and to the point. He writes a factual, descriptive account of the life of Jesus. His simple use of the Greek language means that he uses phrases such as 'at once' and 'immediately' in the recounting of his story. He talks of past events using the present

tense. These stylistic features allow the reader the chance to participate more directly in the story of Jesus' life.

The messianic secret

The 'messianic secret' dominates Mark's portrayal of Jesus. Throughout the gospel Mark shows how Jesus' true identity was not recognised until after his resurrection. The demons recognise Jesus but are ordered to be silent (1.25,34; 3.12). Jesus attempts to avoid publicity for his miracles (1.44; 5.43; 7.36 and 8.26). He often withdrew from the crowds (1.35; 3.7; 9.30) and refused to give a sign to the generation as to his identity (8.12). The secret of Jesus' identity is seen to be intentional on the part of Jesus, and an important theme in Mark's gospel.

We may only guess why it was used by Mark. The secret may be an attempt to explain why the crowds ultimately rejected Jesus and supported the Jewish leaders in their call for his crucifixion. It would also explain why the disciples were so bewildered after Jesus' crucifixion. Although Mark shows how Jesus kept his identity a secret from the people, Mark stresses Jesus' divinity to his readers. The opening verse of the gospel sets the tone for the picture of Jesus which is to follow. Jesus is fully divine, yet fully human.

We have subtitled Mark's portrait of Jesus with the phrase 'Jesus, God's Secret Agent' because of the prominence of the 'messianic secret'. In what ways does Jesus fit the role of a 'secret agent'? The true identity of an agent is only known by a few, and is a closely guarded secret. A secret agent always has a mission to accomplish, and frequently reports on the progress of the mission to a superior. A secret agent may also be very lonely because there is no one able to understand the mission which is being worked on. In these ways, we may see Jesus as God's secret agent. Mark clearly shows us how Jesus' true identity was not recognised, how his mission was not understood, and how despite this, he enjoyed a close relationship with God.

A Note on the Texts Chosen for Study

The texts selected for study appear chronologically in the gospel. As Mark progresses with his account of Jesus' life, his particular concerns and interests become clear. Mark begins by showing Jesus' activities in and around Galilee, then he traces Jesus' move to Jerusalem, and concludes with Jesus' passion in Jerusalem. The selected passages show Jesus' move through Galilee to the confrontation in Jerusalem. The passages, while not arranged thematically, definitely show the multi-faceted person of Jesus which Mark develops. They show a challenging portrait of Jesus, who participated fully in human life and experience. The passages show Jesus' concern with the outcasts and oppressed of society and reflect the attitude and approach which should be adopted by followers of Jesus at all times and in all places — and speak to us directly in our own context here and now.

Ways to use this book within a Bible Study

Each of the studies which follow begin with the full biblical text. The New International Version has been selected as the text which is most accessible for us to use. Following the printed text is a note on other related texts. These may prove useful in that they often show a different perspective on the text being studied. These different perspectives help to define more clearly Mark's specific concerns.

When reading parallel accounts in the gospels, we need to realise that Mark's gospel was written first, and that when the other two differ from Mark, probably the alterations were deliberate. We need to examine the changes and attempt to discover why they were made.

A number of questions which proved helpful to the various groups are then included. Group leaders may find it more useful to use these questions after they have read the exegetical notes on the text, and might perhaps like to add questions of their own.

The purpose of the notes on the text is to explain the meanings of words and ideas which are used in the text. These notes are similar to the approach used in more scholarly commentaries, and as such, serve to comment on the verses in the text.

The reflections on the text all arise out of the studies completed in the various communities already mentioned. They show how the text was read and understood and what people saw them meaning within their own situations. While the reflections are specifically South African in nature, it would be useful for groups to relate them to their own experiences and to the world in which they live.

The discussion of the 'third horizon' was also specifically South Afri-

can in nature, and again groups are encouraged to begin these studies by sketching their own specific horizons. This may be achieved by
discussing the society in which one lives, the economic class which
one belongs to and the political commitments of both the individual
and the country where the study is being done. It is really important
that one carefully examines ones own context, as this will have a pro-
found impact on the readings both of scripture and of the reflections
contained in this book.

Bible Studies

1. Jesus Heals with Authority

Mark 1.21-28

 21 They went to Capernaum, and when the Sabbath came, Jesus went into the synagogue and began to teach.

22 The people were amazed at his teaching, because he taught with authority, not as the teachers of the law.

23 Just then a man in their synagogue who was possessed by an evil spirit cried out,

24 'What do you want with us, Jesus of Nazareth? Have you come to destroy us? I know who you are — the Holy One of God!'

25 'Be quiet!' said Jesus sternly. 'Come out of him!'

26 The evil spirit shook the man violently and came out of him with a shriek.

27 The people were all so amazed that they asked each other, 'What is this? A new teaching — and with authority! He even gives orders to evil spirits and they obey him.'

28 News about him spread quickly over the whole region of Galilee.

Related readings

This is the first recorded healing in Mark's gospel. The account of this healing is not unique to Mark: Matthew implies knowledge of the healing although he does not discuss it or retell it at all (Mt.8.14-17); Luke repeats the story in a manner similar to Mark (Lk.4.31-37). It is useful to read the accounts in the other two gospels, because Mark's special concerns become easier to see.

Questions we may ask of the text

Today, Christians are often faced with the dilemma of which authority they should obey. State authority and God's authority are often in conflict. How should the Christian respond to this situation? The following questions proved useful in discerning the direction which Christians are called to follow:

1   Why were the people amazed at Jesus?
2   How did Jesus' authority differ from that of the scribes?

3 What made Jesus' authority so powerful?
4 How would the Roman Christians (Mark's audience) have understood this clash between two different sorts of authorities?
5 Where today do we witness similar clashes, and how are we as followers of Jesus to respond?

Notes on the text

Mk.1.15 tells us that Jesus had already begun his preaching ministry. He called people to repentance, and declared the good news that God's kingdom had arrived. Mark did not record any of Jesus' earlier sermons, but it seems that Jesus was already a recognised teacher.

Why do we say this? Mark clearly states (1.21) that Jesus entered the synagogue on the sabbath and began to teach. There is no mention of Jesus being invited, or of him asking permission to teach. The tradition of the time held that there was no specific teacher, or Rabbi, at each synagogue. The only permanent official at the synagogue was the *hazzan*, who would read aloud from the law. On the sabbath, people who were renowned for their exposition of the law or for their teaching would read and teach in the synagogue.

This tradition suggests that when Jesus taught at the synagogue in Capernaum, he had already acquired a 'reputation' for his teaching ability. Throughout the gospel, Jesus seems quite at home teaching in synagogues, almost as if he had been trained to do so. The directness and simplicity of v.21 suggests that Jesus had been expected. No one seemed surprised to see Jesus. The astonishment was not directed at his presence, or at what he said, but rather at the way in which he taught.

Although this first miracle took place within a synagogue, the healings in v.29-34 took place within a home and on the streets. What is important about this is the fact that if Jesus had only healed and taught within the confines of the synagogue, only Jewish males would have had access to his teachings and healings. Now, on the other hand, Jesus takes his teachings and healings into the community. Those with whom Jesus mixed included women, people possessed with evil spirits, and probably, even at this stage, non-Jews. In other words, what we see in this first miracle account is that Jesus did not have a selective ministry, but that he was ready to minister to, to teach and to heal all those who approached him.

What is particularly striking in Mark's account of Jesus' first healing miracle, is that the people around Jesus, the crowd, the scribes and even the disciples seem to be completely astonished at Jesus' teachings. At no stage however, are we let into the secret of what it was that Jesus preached on that Sabbath in Capernaum. What is of particular importance to Mark is the manner in which Jesus taught. What seemed to amaze the crowd was that he had authority unlike anyone they had ever encountered.

What does v.22 mean when it says 'he taught with authority and not as the scribes'? The logical place to begin when trying to answer this question is to ask where the scribes derived their authority. It came from the law. They were interpreters of the Jewish law (the Torah), and their main function within the synagogues was to read from it. To work within the law implied that they were bound by and subservient to the law. This is in complete contrast to Jesus. He embodies the law, filling it with new content. The scribes are bound by the law, Jesus is the law.

Perhaps we are not told of the content of the sermon because it was not a new 'radical' teaching, but we are told of the manner in which it was taught because the old message embodied in the Torah now took on a new significance because of the arrival of God's kingdom in Jesus. The law became a living reality, speaking to each individual and challenging each one in a unique way. Mark is continually at pains to show his readers that Jesus sees that the law has been created for people, and not people for the law (read Mk.2.27-28 and Mk.3.4). With his powerful authority, Jesus was freeing all from being a slave to the law, so that they could accept him.

Another important aspect of this story is that the demon alone recognised Jesus and his authority immediately. Jesus however called for silence from the evil spirit. What was the evil spirit, and why did it alone recognise the true identity of Jesus?

The evil spirit correctly viewed Jesus as a threat to his existence, and his attitude is automatically defensive. The words the demoniac utters could well be a reflection of the thoughts and feelings of the crowd. The presence of Jesus is a judgement and call away from the old way of life. Without minimising the power or presence of evil spirits, we could perhaps identify the evil spirit in this story as being symbolic of all forces and people who oppose the form of justice and authority represented by Jesus.

The healing is therefore a vehicle through which Jesus' absolute authority was demonstrated. This challenges us to ask about the implications of Jesus' authority for us today.

Mark must have been aware that this question would be foremost in the mind of his Roman audience. There were two distinct authorities that they were called to obey. The first was the authority of Caesar. Although the various emperors had different opinions of Christianity, some, like Nero, were vehemently opposed. The second authority that they were called to obey was the authority of Jesus, their Lord, which was often in contradiction to that of the Caesar. Mark clearly shows in this passage that Jesus' authority is the one to obey and follow because he had not only verbal authority, like the scribes and learned men, but his authority was God's power over evil. His authority embodied God's will, and was a just authority yet enacted in healing love.

Reflections on the text

Mark's audience, when faced with the dilemma as to whose authority they were to obey, would have had no other option as Christians than to follow God's authority, embodied by Jesus.

The issues of obedience and authority were discussed at length by our study groups because this dilemma of which authority to follow still confronts Christians living in South Africa and elsewhere. The segregation and discrimination, which is legally enforced in South Africa, demands a response from Christians.

Clearly, the groups believed that it is our duty as Christians to obey Christ and follow his example in all things. Because Jesus symbolises and embodies love and justice, it is our duty to work in love towards a just society. We need to examine the authority of the state, which we are called to obey. We need to examine the legitimacy of a state calling itself a Christian state when its racial (or other) laws cannot be condoned or accepted by the Christian church. We are also called to examine the attitude different churches have taken on the political issues facing us. Are the churches merely taking 'comfortable' decisions, or are they really seeking God's direction?

Someone suggested that without recognition, authority is powerless. Authorities only have real power when it is recognised by the people. If people learn to acknowledge and respect the authority rooted in love and justice, and turn away and reject that which is contrary to God's will, the struggle between church and state might begin to be resolved.

We were reminded that the people were amazed at Jesus because he showed them complete authority, authority rooted and love embroiled in action. He liberated all from blindly following rules and showed them a working alternative. This passage offers a challenge to all responsible Christians. We ended the study by reflecting on the following prayer and reading Jeremiah 14.17 - 22.

A prayer for healing

'Gracious Lord, in these troubled times, grant us an awareness of your will, wisdom to know how to respond to your authority, and the courage to face the challenge of adversity. Amen'

2. Faith and Healing

Mark 2.1-12

1 A few days later, when Jesus again entered Capernaum, the people heard that he had come home.

2 So many gathered that there was no room left, not even outside the door, and he preached the Word to them.

3 Some men came, bringing to him a paralytic, carried by four of them.

4 Since they could not get him to Jesus because of the crowd, they made an opening in the roof above Jesus and, after digging through it, lowered the mat the paralysed man was lying on.

5 When Jesus saw their faith, he said to the paralytic, 'Son, your sins are forgiven.'

6 Now some teachers of the law were sitting there, thinking to themselves,

7 'Why does this fellow talk like that? He's blaspheming! Who can forgive sins but God alone?'

8 Immediately Jesus knew in his spirit that this was what they were thinking in their hearts, and he said to them, 'Why are you thinking these things?

9 Which is easier; to say to the paralytic, "Your sins are forgiven," or to say "Get up, take your mat and walk"?

10 But that you may know that the Son of Man has authority on earth to forgive sins. . . .

¹¹ I tell you, get up, take your mat and go home.'
¹² He got up, took his mat and walked out in full view of them all. This amazed everyone and they praised God, saying, 'We have never seen anything like this!'

Related readings

This remarkable account of Jesus healing the paralysed man is also told by Matthew (8.14-17) and Luke (4.38-41). A comparison of these three readings is useful. Although Matthew and Luke include the story, it is Mark's account that is the most vivid. Mark stresses the fullness of the room, the faith of the friends, and the compassion of Jesus.

Questions we may ask of the text

The action of the four friends is extremely relevant for us today. It focusses us on faith in action. A further focal point was the clash with the scribes, who failed to recognise Jesus' authority. The following questions were helpful in opening up the text.

1   Who do you understand the 'their' in verse 5 to refer to?
2   What does this understanding imply about the relationship between sin and suffering?
3   Why were the scribes angry?
4   How would the community in Rome have understood this message?
5   How can we use the message of this text in our lives today?

Notes on the text

There are two important events in this passage. Firstly, Jesus heals a man who is paralysed; secondly, he is accused of blasphemy by the scribes. The issue at stake is not whether healing and forgiveness go hand in hand, but whether Jesus had the authority to forgive or heal.

Jesus' action of forgiving sins before healing the paralytic must be seen against the Old Testament background, where disease and sin are often regarded as corresponding with healing and forgiveness. Healing is often depicted as conditional upon forgiveness from God (eg: Ps.103.3; 2 Chron.7.14 and Is.19.22). The terms 'healing' and 'forgiveness' are even sometimes interchangeable (eg. Ps.41.4; Jer.3.22 and Hos.14.4.). The scribes as well as the crowd would have been aware of this link between the two terms.

Sidney Holo

This understanding clarifies Jesus' explanation for the modern day reader. We should not waste our time debating whether all illness is a result of sin, as this is not implied at all by Jesus or his response to the scribes. The issue at stake is whether Jesus had the authority to heal and forgive. According to the Old Testament, only God had the power to forgive sins. Thus Jesus' statement was seen as an affront to God, and the charge of blasphemy, which was to lead to Jesus' crucifixion, thus began to gather momentum.

Jesus' pronouncement in verse 5 is characteristic of his ministry as portrayed by Mark. It is ambiguous in that it veils his identity yet, in the light of his resurrection, it reveals his self-understanding. Mark wrote from the perspective of the resurrection; yet he describes very forcefully how Jesus was perceived during his life and ministry.

It is characteristic of Mark's gospel that Jesus responds to a conflict situation by posing a counter question (eg. 3.4; 11.30 and 12.37). By questioning the scribes in this manner, Jesus forced them to examine their opposition to him, and showed them how misdirected their anger was.

Verses 5b-10 have posed a problem to scholars. It is unlikely that Jesus would have used the title 'Son of Man' publicly, especially in front of the scribes, so early in his mission. The term is only used after the disciples acknowledge that Jesus is the Messiah (8.29). The disjointed construction of the verses suggest that v.5b - 10 are Mark's interpretation of the healing. He used this first healing to make an important theological point about the nature of Jesus. Verse 10a is a probably a statement addressed specifically to the Roman Christians, showing the relevance of the healing for them; the word 'you' could refer to the scribes, but it seems more likely that it refers to the Christians living in Rome.

Verse 12 concludes the passage effectively as Jesus' authority is again shown to be rooted in action. The criticism and condemnation of the scribes was halted when they witnessed the power of Jesus.

Reflections on the text

In our group discussions, we considered the important role played by the four friends who carried the paralysed man. They acted on behalf of one who could not help himself, and their action was one of selfless giving. They expected no accolades or thanks, and seem to disappear into the crowd after the healing. It is their faith, moreover, which leads to their friend's healing. These friends were seen to represent the community of caring so central to the Christian life.

We found that in our group many people felt exhausted, lost or directionless. People in this situation need to be carried by the Christian community. There are also times when we have to recognise our dependence on others and accept the help they offer out of loving concern for us. It is not enough merely to accept their help, rather, it is essential to use it as a starting point for positive action. Just as in the story the lame man was ordered to walk, so too those who are supported by others are called to take definitive action toward ultimately helping themselves. People need to recognise their weaknesses, and allow others to help them.

In Rome, the Christian church was struggling against persecution. Many of its members belonged to the lower income group, which meant that they were facing unemployment and high taxation. It is the duty of Christians to be aware of others in the community who may need their help, and then help them until they are able to cope more fully.

Another important aspect of this story is the action of the crowd. The crowd was so busy listening to Jesus that they failed to see what was happening around them. How often Christians today are like that crowd. Christians become so intent upon focussing on Jesus and his word, that they neglect the issues and concerns of others - which are so important to Jesus.

There were two different types of people in this story. One group turned their backs on others and this kept them from Jesus; the other displayed love in action and brought their friend to a point of healing. It is the action of this group, the friends, which Jesus commends.

One challenge which this passage offers to Christians living in South Africa and elsewhere is that they should be aware of the danger of becoming complacent in their faith. They should continually be aware of others around them who may need their help or attention. Any faith in Jesus demands corresponding action, and when one acts in faith, Jesus responds accordingly.

This passage would also have clarified the issue of authority for the Christians in Rome. The scribes did not acknowledge Jesus' authority and were critical of his words and deeds, yet Jesus is shown to have ultimate authority. Healing proceeds from him. Authority rooted in laws is again shown to be subservient to the authority of Jesus, displayed by love in action.

How do you respond to authority today?

A prayer of confession

The focus of our reflections has shown us how we are to be more like the four friends, displaying love and caring leading to healing. Seeing their example, many people in the group realised that we all fall short of what is expected of us. We felt the need to express our inadequacies, and closed the group by reading together this prayer of confession:

Leader: Oh Lord, we have not loved you with our whole heart and mind and strength;

People: we have not loved our neighbours as ourselves;
we have not forgiven others as we have been forgiven.

Leader: We have often been deaf to your call to serve as Christ served us;

People: we have not had in us the mind of Christ;
we have grieved your Holy Spirit.

Leader: Accept our repentance Lord, for the wrongs we have done:

People: for our blindness to human need and suffering, and our indifference to injustice and cruelty;
for our prejudice and contempt toward those who differ from us;
for our waste and abuse of your creation, and our lack of concern for those who come after us.

Leader: Restore us, good Lord, and let your anger turn from us.

People: Hear us for your mercy is great.

Leader: Accomplish in us the the work of your salvation,

People: That we may show forth your glory in the world.

Pause

Unison: The Lord is tender and compassionate; slow to anger, most loving;
no less than the height of heaven over earth is the greatness of the love of the Lord;
as far as the east is from the west, so far have our sins and transgressions been removed from us.
Thank you Lord. Amen.

3. Jesus Eats with Sinners

Mark 2.13-17

¹³ Once again Jesus went out beside the lake. A large crowd came to him and he began to teach them.

¹⁴ As he walked along, he saw Levi, son of Alphaeus sitting at the tax collector's booth. 'Follow me,' Jesus told him, and Levi got up and followed him.

¹⁵ While Jesus was having dinner at Levi's house, many tax collectors and 'sinners' were eating with him and his disciples, for there were many who followed him.

¹⁶ When the teachers of the law who were the Pharisees saw him eating with the 'sinners' and tax collectors, they asked his disciples: 'Why does he eat with tax collectors and 'sinners'?

¹⁷ On hearing this, Jesus said to them, 'It is not the healthy who need a doctor, but the sick. I have not come to call the righteous, but sinners.'

Related readings

All three of the synoptic gospels include the account of Levi's call and Jesus' meal with the tax collectors and 'sinners' (Mt.9.9-13; Lk.5.27-32). Although the three accounts are similar, a reading of all three versions proves useful. An interesting difference in the three accounts lies in the naming of Levi or Matthew. The gospel of Matthew speaks of the calling of Matthew, Luke speaks of Levi and Mark tells his readers that Levi was the son of Alphaeus. Marks' precision in naming is a common feature of the second gospel.

Questions we may ask of the text

The nature of the sinners and of the tax collectors' profession is relevant to the understanding of this passage. Jesus' response to the antagonism of the scribes is also an important area for discussion. The study groups examined these issues together with the following questions in order to get a better understanding of what the text is saying today.

1 What is distinctive about Levi's call?
2 Why does Mark specifically mention the sort of people that Jesus was sharing his meal with?
3 Who did Jesus imply when he used the terms 'righteous' and 'sinners'?

Sidney Holo

4   How can we understand 'tax collectors' today, and what should be our response to these people?

Notes on the text

After the dramatic healing of the paralysed man (2.1 - 12), Jesus withdrew to the sea. Here he makes the dramatic call to Levi, the tax collector. Mark does not tell us why Jesus withdrew, and he tells us little about Levi. Mark's concern is rather with the radical nature of Levi's call.

Levi would have been a Jewish tax collector in the service of Herod Antipas. Tax officials were loathed and despised by the community because of the huge sums they extorted from the people over and above the level of tax demanded by the state. The position of tax and customs officials was leased to contenders; once they had covered the cost of the lease all the money they raised was their profit. When a Jew entered this profession he was regarded as an outcast from society. He was disqualified as a judge or even as a witness in court, and he was excommunicated from the synagogue. His family was also disgraced and cast out by the community.

Levi worked in the tax office in Capernaum, a place where Jesus had spent much time. Levi would certainly have heard of Jesus before being encountered by the call. One thing which makes this call more dramatic is that Levi probably knew the fishermen who accompanied Jesus, as he would have been responsible for taxing them. It must have been extremely difficult for Jesus' followers to have understood why Jesus had called such a man, especially one whom they knew and despised. Levi's call shows how Jesus extends grace to society's outcasts. Levi obediently follows Jesus' command, and his joy is evident when he invites Jesus and his friends to share in a meal at his home.

The term 'sinners' should not be understood as implying one who does not obey God. Rather, the word refers to those whom the Pharisees understood as being sinners. In the eyes of the Pharisees, sinners were those who showed no interest in the scribal tradition and who were thus deemed inferior. As used by the scribes and Pharisees, the term 'sinners' would be equivalent to 'outcasts'. These people would not have observed the standard rituals of cleanliness before eating and, by eating with them, Jesus would also be regarded as unclean. The Pharisees avoided all contact with such people as any contact would imply ritual impurity on their part.

The Pharisees regarded Jesus as a teacher and one well versed in the Law. This makes his action incomprehensible to them. It was seen as a disgrace that a teacher should be sharing a meal with these people.

Jesus immediately recognises their antagonism, and responds in a manner which they would understand. He uses a well known proverb which the Pharisees would have recognised and understood. Jesus does not deny that the people are sinners, but rather adopts the form of logical argument used by the Pharisees to show where his true mission lay. Again, the difference between the Pharisees and Jesus is in their interpretation of the law.

Reflections on the text

The actions of Jesus speak very clearly to many Christians living in South Africa and elsewhere. Jesus intentionally moved out of 'acceptable' company and mixed with those whom society condemned. Who are the people condemned by society today? Who fills a similar position to the tax collectors in today's society?

The literal tax collectors of today are those who work for the revenue service and these people are certainly no longer regarded as outcasts. Various communities have different types of people who they believe have let down the rest of the community. Clearly, Christians should interact with these people.

The 'coloured' congregation who assisted with this study believe that they were let down by members of their community who joined parliament in the new Tri-cameral political system. They believe that these people have joined the ruling class for financial reasons and prestige. While this might not always be the case, the anger of the community must be respected.

The Christian message requires that these people are not cast out but instead confronted by the challenge of Jesus. When Levi was called he did not continue working as a customs official, but rather began to follow Jesus. Responding to Jesus' call implies a change in life style.

The text also shows how Christians need to mix with those who are rejected by others. Christians need to follow Jesus' example and move out of 'accepted' circles to share with others. The groups spent time discussing which community Jesus would work with if he lived in South Africa, or elsewhere in the world, today. Would he spend time with Christians who believed that because they were 'saved' they need not waste time with those who clearly did not know the truth? Such Christians believe that their faith is sufficient and that they are superior to others. Jesus' actions speak directly to these people. He shows how self-righteousness is wrong and that people should act in a way which reflects their faith.

The groups realised that we should not point fingers and judge others, but as Christians we need to be aware that Jesus calls all people.

When did you last eat with a prostitute?

4. The People's Understanding of Jesus

Mark 8.27-33

27 Jesus and his disciples went on to the villages around Caesarea Philippi. On the way he asked them, 'Who do people say I am?'

28 They replied, 'Some say John the Baptist; others say Elijah; and still others, one of the prophets.'

29 'But what about you?' he asked. 'Who do you say I am?' Peter answered, 'You are the Christ.'

30 Jesus warned them not to tell anyone about him.

31 He then began to teach them that the Son of Man must suffer many things and be rejected by the elders, chief priests and teachers of the law, and that he must be killed and after three days rise again.

32 He spoke plainly about this, and Peter took him aside and began to rebuke him.

33 But when Jesus turned and looked at his disciples, he rebuked Peter. 'Out of my sight, Satan!' he said. 'You do not have in mind the things of God, but the things of men.

Questions we may ask of the text

We began our studies by showing how this passage marks a watershed in the gospel, and how Peter's confession is central to the structure of Mark's gospel. Until this point Jesus had travelled throughout the area and his power and teaching had amazed the people. Although the people marvelled at Jesus, they did not recognise his true identity. Now, Jesus asks what people are saying about him. Following Peter's confession, Jesus at last reveals to his disciples the suffering that he is to go through.

The following questions proved useful to us in coming to a clearer understanding of the disciples' understanding of Jesus, in comparison to Jesus' self-understanding.

1   In what ways does Jesus seem 'different' in this passage?
2   Compare the title which Jesus gives himself to those that the disciples have given him.
3   Do you think that the disciples really understood who Jesus was? (Explain your answer carefully.)
4   How would the disciples have understood v.31, and how do we deal with similar confusions today?

Notes on the text

This passage is an example of the many instances where Mark precedes a teaching of Jesus with a question. Here, the purpose of the first question is to prepare for the more personal question which Jesus poses to the disciples in v.29. Mark shows how the disciples' understanding of Jesus' identity was more developed than that of the crowds but that his full identity is hidden both from the crowds and from his disciples. Until this point, only the demons had recognised Jesus and they had been ordered to remain silent. Now, Jesus reveals his identity and his mission to the disciples. Yet again, he calls the disciples to remain silent about what he was about to reveal to them.

The identification of Jesus with John the Baptist and Elijah shows that many people only understood him to be another messenger of God. This understanding denies the unique identity and mission of Jesus. But Peter, speaking on behalf of the disciples, confirms his faith in Jesus in a new and ultimately decisive way, even though he did not fully understand what he was saying.

Peter identifies Jesus as 'the Christ' or 'the Messiah', meaning, 'the anointed one of God'. This title shows that the disciples understood that Jesus had been elected and blessed by God, and that as a result he had special divine powers. While the disciples recognised divine blessing resting on Jesus, it seems unlikely that they realised the full implications of Jesus' understanding of Messiahship.

The Jews were expecting a Messiah, one who would follow in David's line (2 Sam.7.14 - 16). They expected a Messiah who would deliver them from the Romans. Jesus, however, had a different understanding of the phrase. Jesus saw this misunderstanding and proceeded to teach the disciples about his understanding of Messiahship.

It was vital that the disciples understood what Messiahship implied for Jesus. Jesus in fact does not acknowlege Peter's understanding of Messiah. Instead, he speaks of himself as the 'Son of Man'. Jesus prefers to use this title when describing himself. While he speaks in the third person of 'the Son of Man', this is not because he identified the title with someone else — rather this was in keeping with Mark's idea of the 'Messianic Secret'. The title 'Son of Man' has been shown to be an Aramaic idiom, which could be understood as meaning 'I'. The idiom usually occurred in sentences which implied a meaning of humiliation and suffering, and was thus particularly appropriate for Jesus' self-understanding.

Peter rebuked Jesus because Jesus' self-understanding was completely different from that of the disciples. Their understanding was of someone who would release them from the bondage of the Romans. Jesus however shows that this is not his intention and that on the contrary, he is going to suffer and to die. This would have been an enigma to the disciples.

Mark uses the term 'Son of Man' fourteen times: twelve of these occur after Peter's confession, and usually refer to the suffering and humiliation which Jesus is to experience. Jesus' use of the term shows how he had accepted the inevitable shame which was to follow.

In the way that Jesus answers these questions, we can see how Mark used the questioning of the disciples as a foil for the faith of the Christians living in Rome

When Jesus rebukes Peter, one is made aware that the disciples have still not grasped the full implications of Jesus' statement. They are still incredulous about Jesus' destiny. Jesus' message, as understood by the disciples, was not completely negative, but rather, the promise of the resurrection was central to Jesus' self-disclosure.

Reflections on the text

As Christians we often misunderstand the implications of our Christianity. Like the disciples, we fail to listen to what Jesus said.

In the groups we discussed how Jesus shows that suffering and humiliation are central to the Christian experience. In the verses which follow the passage (8.34 - 9.1) Jesus elaborates on his understanding of the suffering which those who decide to follow him must experience. The Christian life may sometimes be very comfortable, with Christians not being prepared to take a stand for their faith. But Jesus clearly speaks out against this attitude. Christianity implies taking a stand, even if this leads to persecution or death.

South Africa claims to be a Christian country, and it uses the Bible as a basis of the constitution and as a legitimisation for the practise of apartheid. Clearly the Bible is being misused. Christians are called to respond to this situation, and to speak out against the heretical use of the Bible. Responding in this manner may invoke the anger of the state and even of other Christians, but if one truly believes that an injustice is being perpetrated, then one is obliged to respond accordingly.

Jesus was aware of the hardships he was to suffer, yet this did not discourage him. In the face of adversity, Jesus did not back down. Christians need to recognise the very real threat of antagonism and opposition, and to stand firm with their faith despite the response of others. A source of strength for Christians is the knowlege that they are not alone: and that they are supported by Jesus and his call for justice.

Just as the disciples could not tell Jesus how he was to lead them, so we cannot prescribe the form of Christianity which we find it comfortable to follow. Christianity calls for its adherents to follow Jesus in both his teachings and his love. Although the example which Jesus set may be difficult to emulate, to follow Jesus is not an option but a command!

The groups reflected on the words of Dietrich Bonhoeffer, who once said 'When Christ calls a man, he bids him come and die.' We linked these words of Bonhoeffer with the words of Jesus in Mark 8.35 '. . . whoever loses his life for me and for the gospel will save it.' The immensity of the call to follow Jesus soon became clear to all.

We then turned to reflect on the things which held us back from following Jesus in the true sense. One group suggested writing these things down, and then burning the paper as a symbol of releasing ourselves from the many things hindering us in our Christian life.

After closing in prayer, many people in the groups felt a renewed commitment to Jesus and the life to which they had been called.

5. The Transfiguration: A New Beginning

Mark 9.2-8

2   After six days Jesus took Peter, James and John with him and led them up a high mountain, where they were all alone. There he was transfigured before them.

3   His clothes became dazzling white, whiter than anyone in the world could bleach them.

4   And there appeared before them Elijah and Moses, who were talking with Jesus.

5   Peter said to Jesus, 'Rabbi, it is good for us to be here. Let us put up three shelters — one for you, one for Moses and one for Elijah.'

6   (He did not know what to say, they were so frightened.)

7   Then a cloud appeared and enveloped them, and a voice came from the cloud: 'This is my Son, whom I love. Listen to him.'

8   Suddenly, when they looked round, they no longer saw anyone with them except Jesus.

Questions we may ask of the text

Mark at last shows his readers the true nature of Jesus and his mission. The transfiguration passage follows on from Peter's confession. It shows how Jesus' explanation of his nature and mission has become a reality. The study groups came to a better understanding of the text after working through the following questions.

1   How does Mk 8.27-38 prepare us as readers for the transfiguration event?

2   Discuss this passage in relation to 8.38.

3   What is Mark disclosing to his readers about Jesus and his mission?

4   Do Peter and the others realise the importance of this event?
5   What is the importance of the reported presence of Moses and
      Elijah?

Notes on the text

Jesus' transfiguration serves as a demonstration of God's divine
approval, and as a blessing on the persecution which he was to
experience. The transfiguration also confirms Jesus' prophecy of his
ultimate vindication. The revelation also finds a close parallel to the
voice heard at Jesus' baptism (1.9-11), showing God's approval of
Jesus thoughout his mission.

The reference to the six days which passed between Jesus' self-disclosure and the transfiguration recalls an Old Testament tradition.
Ex.24.16f shows how six days is a period of preparation before a revelation. Mark thus uses this understanding as a basis for his account.

Peter, James and John often share a privileged relationship with
Jesus (5.37; 13.3 and 14.33), and their presence at the transfiguration
allows them to witness Jesus' glory. Their presence also serves to
remind us of Jesus' words in 9.1, when he prophesies that some of his
disciples will witness the power of the kingdom of God before they
die. The link between the two passages and their interrelatedness
can easily be seen.

In the transfiguration, Mark gives his readers a glimpse of the divine
nature of Jesus, who has until this point appeared to be fully human.
Mark has always stressed how Jesus identifies with humanity
because he was fully human too. Now, however, his divinity is also
clearly attested. The human Jesus is changed before the eyes of his
closest disciples as they are offered a glimpse of the glory which Jesus
was to experience after the persecution. They witness a dis-
closure of God's plan to vindicate Jesus from his suffering.

Moses and Elijah are present at the transfiguration as witnesses prepared to testify to his character and mission. Moses represents the
old law and covenant which the Jews had with God, and Elijah is
seen as the prophet who restores all things (1.2f; 9.11). In Jesus, the
promise of the second exodus has become a reality: Jesus is the new
covenant and the new law. Elijah's presence shows that all is now to
be fulfilled. The transfiguration serves as a very important prelude to
the passion events, for it allows us to realise the ultimate end which is

in sight for Jesus throughout the suffering of the passion.

Peter's impulsive response to what he had witnessed was typical of his character thus far in the gospel. His response shows how the disciples were not aware of the full significance of that which they had witnessed. Their desire to erect tents may be traced back to the Old Testament phenomenon of conversing with God in tents. It seems as if the three presumed that the promised glory of Jesus had now been realised and that the suffering which he had prophesied was no longer to be expected. This again shows their basic misunderstanding of the transfiguration event and the approaching passion.

The Old Testament often has a cloud covering the majesty of God (Ex.16.10; 19.9, 33.1). Once again, Mark shows the link between the religion of the Old Testament and the new religion which is now fulfilled in Jesus. God's response to Peter is important as it signifies divine approval and commands utter obedience to Jesus. This call to obey Jesus reminds us of Deut.18.15, where Israel is commanded to follow the final bearer of God's word.

After the cloud lifts, Jesus is left alone, Moses and Elijah have disappeared. Jesus had been given support and encouragement and now, with this renewed strength, he has to go forth to face the passion. The disciples who witnessed the event were confused as to its significance and so Jesus could not even depend on them for support, he has to face the future alone.

Reflections on the text

How is one to relate to the events of the transfiguration today? It is easy to identify with the confusion of the disciples, who had still not perceived the true identity of their leader. Today, we view the story of the transfiguration after the event of the resurrection, so it is easier to recognise the true nature of Jesus. We know that Jesus was blessed by God and that his mission was divinely approved, yet the confusion experienced by the disciples is still real for us today.

How often are Christians today led by a misdirected sense of what is expected of them? We realised how God's words to Peter, 'Listen to him', are still relevant today. Christians need to be still and to listen to Jesus. While Christians today may not be able to hear Jesus literally, his actions two thousand years ago still dictate the path that Christians should follow.

When Jesus received divine approval, his actions were naturally approved of too. Christians need to examine Jesus' actions carefully, and to place these actions in the context of their daily life and experiences. The teachings, works and actions of Jesus are not restricted to the situation which he was working with, but rather, are relevant for all today. Although each situation called for a different response, God clearly supported Jesus in his quest for justice and his display of love. It is this same call for love and justice which should motivate Christians today.

The command to listen to Jesus certainly applies to all that Jesus taught, but more specifically to the advice which Jesus gave to his disciples about the necessity of suffering for his name. Clearly this suffering is part of God's plan too, and Christians today who suffer as a result of their faith may draw support from this knowlege.

The event of the transfiguration is important today as Christians face the same dilemmas and problems as the disciples did. We may view the transfiguration as an account which proves God's support for Jesus and his mission, as well as for the call and demands which the Christian faith makes on its adherents.

6. Jesus' Despair and a Call to Faith

Mark 9.14-29

14 When they came to the other disciples, they saw a large crowd around them and the teachers of the law arguing with them.

15 As soon as all the people saw Jesus, they were overwhelmed with wonder and ran to greet him.

16 'What are you arguing with them about?' he asked.

17 A man in the crowd answered, 'Teacher, I brought you my son, who is possessed by a spirit that has robbed him of speech.

18 Whenever it seizes him, it throws him to the ground. He nashes his teeth and becomes rigid. I asked your disciples to drive out the spirit, but they could not.'

19 'O unbelieving generation,' Jesus replied, 'how long shall I stay with you? How long shall I put up with you? Bring the boy to me.'

²⁰ So they brought him. When the spirit saw Jesus, it immediately threw the boy into a convulsion. He fell to the ground and rolled around, foaming at the mouth.

²¹ Jesus asked the boy's father, 'How long has he been like this?' 'From childhood,' he answered.

²² 'It has often thrown him into the fire or water to kill him. But if you can do anything, take pity on us and help us.'

²³ 'If you can?' said Jesus. 'Everything is possible for him who believes.'

²⁴ Immediately the boy's father exclaimed , 'I do believe; help me overcome my unbelief!'

²⁵ When Jesus saw that a crowd was returning to the scene, he rebuked the evil spirit. 'You deaf and dumb spirit,' he said, 'I command you, come out of him and never enter him again.'

²⁶ The spirit shrieked, convulsed him violently and came out. The boy looked so much like a corpse that many said, 'He's dead.'

²⁷ But Jesus took him by the hand and lifted him to his feet, and he stood up.

²⁸ After Jesus had gone indoors, his disciples asked him privately, 'Why couldn't we drive it out?'

²⁹ He replied, 'This kind can come out only by prayer.'

Related readings

Mark's account of this event is far more detailed and vivid than either Matthew's (17.14-20) or Luke's(Lk.9.37-43), and v.21-4 and 26-27 are not included by the others. The crowd's amazement and the sympathy and love shown by Jesus are clearly demonstrated by Mark. A close reading of these three texts will assist us in understanding the way in which Mark's gospel seems to be offering an 'eye-witness' account of the events. The way that Mark writes allows the reader to understand the feelings of all those involved far more clearly.

Questions we may ask of the text

As we worked through the following questions we began to understand the heart of the text's message.

1   Why were crowds amazed when they saw Jesus?

2   What does Jesus' question in v.21 tell us of Mark's understanding of Jesus?

3   How would the Roman community, and Christians today, respond to the message of v.23 -24?

4   What does this passage tell us about Jesus' continual battle with (1) evil forces and (2) lack of faith?

Hamilton K. Budaza

Notes on the text

The passage seems to be written from the perspective of one of the disciples returning from the mountain after the transfiguration. A sharp contrast between the glory of Jesus and the reality of demon possession is drawn by Mark. The powerlessness of the disciples may be seen as a result of their failure to truly understand Jesus and his mission.

The people's astonishment at seeing Jesus is important to observe. Fear and astonishment are often recorded in Mark's gospel and they serve to emphasise a moment of revelation. In this passage, Jesus reveals the importance of prayer and faith, without which one is rendered powerless.

The father of the possessed boy brought his son to Jesus because he expected deliverance. Jesus' reputation had obviously spread throughout the area. The radical nature of the boy's possession shows how the intent of demon possession is to distort and even destroy the image of God in men and women.

The boy had been brought to the disciples because it was understood that they had the same power as their leader, and in Jesus' absence the disciples' responsibility was to heal the boy. They had been commanded by Jesus to expel demons and had been successful (6.7,13). The disciples had exercised this power before, but now that Jesus was away, they had lost the necessary faith.

Jesus' words in v.19 are extremely moving. The exasperation which Jesus experienced as a result of his disciples' lack of faith is an emotion which is fully human. The words are addressed to the disciples who have failed Jesus, but also include the crowds who claim to believe in Jesus, yet lose faith when left alone. Jesus' cry is that of one alone and in anguish. He is completely alone because he has been utterly let down by those whom he believed in. The experiences of the disciples might also be seen as referring directly to the Christians living in Rome. The words can be seen as encouraging those who feel incapable and weak. They are now commanded to remain within their faith.

When Jesus asks the father how long his son had suffered, Jesus' humanity and compassion for the world can be seen. The love that Mark had for Jesus is clearly attested to when we read these 'personal glimpses' of Jesus.

Jesus shows how healing is dependent on faith, and the father recognises this and realises that his faith is insufficient and that only Jesus can assist him. The cry of the father is one from the heart, it is a cry of helplessness and of a desire to attain faith. Jesus automatically responds to the father, knowing how desperate he was. Jesus healed the boy when he noticed that a crowd was beginning to gather. This is typical of other healings in Mark where Jesus attempts to hide his identity.

The epilogue to the account is essential in that it explains to the disciples — and the readers — why they had failed in their attempts to heal. Jesus shows the necessity of faith and prayer working together. He shows his disciples that each occasion they are called on to heal demands prayer, and that they cannot presume success without prayer, merely because they had healed before.

Reflections on the text

This account speaks clearly to Christians today, living without the physical presence of Jesus. The Christians in Rome would also have found comfort in the passage as they too were experiencing life without the daily guidance of Jesus in person.

The passage is a challenge to all who feel despondent and helpless. Today, Christians are confronted with demon possession and evil in many different forms. Just as it was the duty of the disciples to respond in prayer and action to this evil, so too is it the duty of Christians today to respond similarly.

The Christians in Rome were being persecuted for their faith, and in this passage Mark commands them not to give up but to fight back. Jesus shows how action based in prayer and faith is what is expected of those who choose to follow him.

Today, Christians in South Africa and elsewhere are no longer necessarily persecuted for what they believe, but rather for the actions which their faith calls them to take. Just as the teachers of the law attempted to show the weaknesses of the disciples, people today still point accusatory fingers at Christians. Christians are often viewed as being weak and powerless because they do not demonstrate faith in action. It is the duty of Christians to show that the power demonstrated by Jesus is still available to all today.

The message this passage offers to Christians living in difficult times is that they are not to give up and submit to the evils in the world, but rather, they are to go forward in prayer and faith and claim the promise of support which Jesus makes.

One Bible study group had this very meaningful interpretation of the text. The support which Jesus offers to those who are alone was seen as being experienced by the many Christians who are in detention in South Africa today. These people have been persecuted because of the actions which their faith demands. It is to these people, suffering because of their faith, that Jesus will give the strength necessary to remain faithful.

One of the most important supports that we as Christians may enjoy is the Christian community — the people with whom we share a common faith and commitment. In the study groups we realised how important it was for us to recognise our need and dependence on each other.

Group prayer
We closed the groups by reading this passage together:

Leader: Bless the Lord, my soul and all that is within me.
People: Bless the Lord, my soul, and remember the Lord's kindness.
Leader: In calling you out of darkness, and bringing you into the light of friendship;
People: in surrounding us with friends in faith, and providing us with love to share;
Leader: in redeeming you from times of separation;
People: in bringing us into union with others;
Leader: in granting you power to destroy walls that divide;
People: in opening doors to self-knowledge through the gifts of our friends.
Leader: The Lord does what is right and is always on the side of the isolated and lonely;
People: the Lord has brought us into community, and has called together the lonely of the earth.
Leader: The Lord is tender and compassionate, slow to anger and most loving;
People: So will we be treated by the most loving Lord.
Leader: It is the Lord who has brought you into fullness of life.
People: It is the Lord who has healed our brokenness;

Leader: it is the Lord who has brought you in touch with one
        another;
People: it is the Lord who has shown us how to be together.
Unison: Bless the Lord, all you who know life,
        bless the Lord, you who celebrate one another,
        bless the Lord, all you who share a covenant of joy,
        bless the Lord my soul.

7. Jesus' Teaching on Riches

Mark 10.17-31

17 As Jesus started on his way, a man ran up to him and fell on his knees before him. 'Good teacher,' he asked, 'what must I do to inherit eternal life?'

18 'Why do you call me good?' Jesus answered. 'No one is good — except God alone.

19 You know the commandments: Do not murder, do not commit adultery, do not steal, do not give false testimony, do not defraud, honour your father and mother.'

20 'Teacher,' he declared, 'All these have I kept since I was a boy.'

21 Jesus looked at him and loved him. 'One thing you lack,' he said, 'Go, sell everything you have and give to the poor, and you will have treasure in heaven. Then come, follow me.'

22 At this the man's face fell. He went away sad, because he had great wealth.

23 Jesus looked around and said to his disciples, 'How hard it is for a rich man to enter the kingdom of God!'

24 The disciples were amazed at his words. But Jesus said again, 'Children, how hard it is to enter the kingdom of God! It is easier for a camel to go through the eye of a needle than for a rich man to enter the kingdom of God.'

26 The disciples were even more amazed and said to each other, 'Who then can be saved?'

27 Jesus looked at them and said, 'With man this is impossible, but not with God; all things are possible with God.'

28 Peter said to him, 'We have left everything to follow you!'

29 'I tell you the truth,' Jesus replied, 'no one who has left home or brothers or sisters or mother or father or children or fields for me and the gospel

30 will fail to receive a hundred times as much in this present age

(homes, brothers, sisters, mothers, children and fields — and with them persecutions) and in the age to come, eternal life.
31 But many who are first will be last, and the last first.'

Questions we may ask of the text

Having examined a number of Jesus' activities aand miracles, it is important to examine his words and see what he taught his disciples. Jesus' teachings on riches are firm and cannot be disputed. However, people often misunderstand this important teaching, and this mis-understanding needs to be cleared up so that we might be truly challenged by the message of the text. A reading of the other two synoptic accounts (Mt.19.16-30; Lk.18-30) would be useful before working through the following questions.

1   Why does the young man call Jesus 'good teacher'?
2   Why does Jesus call his disciples 'children'?
3   What criticism is Jesus levelling at society through this passage?
4   Who is Mark directing this passage at?
5   How is one to understand v.30 -31?
6   What 'riches' do we possess that might hinder us from following Jesus?

Notes on the text

This text reflects the understanding of self-denial necessary in following Jesus (8.34-38; 9.33-37). The call to follow Jesus means trusting him implicitly. This trust which is expected of Christians means that there is no room for love of money or any other material things.

The question addressed to Jesus in v.17 seems to suggest that the young man believed that inheritance of eternal life was wholly dependent on the works of the individual and that there was no room for divine grace. This is reminiscent of the Old Testament understanding, where good works are crucial to attaining salvation.

The young man tells Jesus how he has obeyed the commandments to the letter, but obviously he feels no security within his religion, hence his approach to Jesus. Jesus senses his concerns and invites the man to follow him. Jesus shows how obedience to the commandments is insufficient, self-surrender to Jesus himself is what is required.

The call which Jesus makes to the young man is particular to this situ-

Hamilton K. Budaza

ation. The young man had clearly put his faith in his riches and earthly belongings, and in giving them up, he would demonstrate ultimate faith in Jesus. Jesus is not saying that wealth is evil or wrong, but rather that the love of money corrupts people and is wrong.

The idea of 'treasure in heaven' reflects an understanding of a Jewish idiom. When Jesus uses these idiomatic expressions, the scribes would have been able to understand the implications of his message clearly.

On hearing what was required of him, the young man was disappointed and realised that he could not respond adequately. Jesus calls those who would follow him to leave anything that they might value above their discipleship, whether this be family, friends or wealth. When one follows Jesus, all ties to other things which might hold one back must be cast away.

Jesus' response to the rich man shows that even those who earnestly might wish to follow Jesus become too attached to earthly belongings. Jesus was also speaking directly to those who believed that their wealth was a sign of God's favour. The Sadducees were amongst this group. Jesus shows that love of wealth will interfere with any decision to follow him. In Judaism this understanding would have been impossible, because riches were clearly a sign of God's favour (eg Job 1.10, Ps.128.2). Jesus shows how wealth might help to create a false sense of security, while real security is attained through faith in Jesus.

Again, the disciples were amazed at Jesus' words: they still did not understand him or his mission. Jesus notes their amazement, and compounds it by illustrating his message with a reference to the largest of the animals known to them — the camel — and the tiny eye of a needle. The love and mercy of God can overcome even this seeming impossibility.

Peter again speaks on behalf of the group, trying to show Jesus that they have sacrificed all for him. Jesus responds by reminding the disciples of the persecution which they are to expect. It is not enough to make these sacrifices and expect all to go well, persecution is to be anticipated. The persecution will be rewarded however, not on earth, where rewards are useless, but rather in heaven. Anyone who suffers for their faith or for actions which result from following Jesus, will ultimately gain from this experience. This is the promise and assurance of Jesus.

The final verse, v.31, may be understood in two ways. It might refer to the fact that though we are persecuted and cast out by society in the present age, this will be reversed in the time to come. It is thus a statement of consolation and promise. It could, however, be a warning. The disciples — and others — who believe that through their actions of sacrifice they are special and above reproach, may be being warned against complacency. They are not to become proud and boastful like the pharisees, because this would result in losing their final 'rewards' or acknowlegement.

Jesus thus calls for complete commitment and sacrifice, but all are to realise that this cannot ultimately guarantee salvation, because this will always be through the grace of God.

Reflections on the text

While this text speaks directly about riches and the correct attitude to have about them, riches may be understood to mean a number of things. Riches are symbolic of any barrier which hinders people from sacrificing all to follow Jesus.

We may hold many things as being central to our lives. It might be a sense of success or prestige, perhaps a position held in society or money itself. All these desires will stop us from following the commands implicit in the Christian life. If we do hold these achievements as particularly central to our lives, then they will become more important than the Christian life. It is thus the desire that the Christian life be central in our life which is the message this passage offers us.

In what ways might these desires be detrimental to the Christian life? Christianity implies action in faith, and this action may seem threatening to one who values their prestige or financial position. Clearly, nothing should interfere with fulfilling the commands of Jesus. It is important that everyone evaluates their lives in order to see if anything would hinder them in following the demands of Christianity. If anything is held to be more dear than the Christian life, then it needs to be confronted and worked through in order that Jesus may again become the top priority.

The text is not specifically against worldly possessions, but rather it speaks against the love of these possessions. It does not seem as if Jesus is deploring worldly goods, but rather the love of these goods. Certainly, if one is wealthy, then one has an added responsibility to use the wealth towards the furthering of God's kingdom. The means by which one comes by wealth should also be examined, and money gained through the exploitation or oppression of others is clearly going against the will of God.

The challenge set to us through this text is that Jesus calls for the Christian faith and life to be set as a priority, and that anything which gets in the way of this call should be cast away.

Is there anything blocking our Christian witness? If so, let us turn from it and re-embrace the Christian message in its entirety.

8. The New Religion Versus the Old

Mark 11.15-18

 15 On reaching Jerusalem, Jesus entered the Temple area and began driving out those who were buying and selling there. He overturned the tables of the money changers and the benches of those selling doves,

16 and would not allow anyone to carry merchandise through the Temple courts.

17 And as he taught them, he said, 'Is it not written: "My house will be called a house of prayer for all nations." But you have made it a "den of robbers".'

18 The chief priests and the teachers of the law heard this and began looking for a way to kill him, for they feared him, because the whole crowd was amazed at his teaching.

Related readings

Before proceeding with a study of v.15-18, it would be useful to read v.1-19 as well as the accounts offered by Matthew (21.12,13), Luke (19.45,46) and John (2.13-17). Mark's account is not as detailed as John's but seems to be an eye-witness account, containing many details.

Questions we may ask of the text

This passage was studied by the groups in late November, at the same time as the shops were being decked out with Christmas decorations. The contrast between the joviality of the 'festive season' and the harsh reality of South Africa, labouring under the second State of Emergency, was immense. The reflections on this text show the confusion and even anger in the hearts of many Christians. Although the reflections dwell specifically upon Christmas, other groups may find the following questions useful in highlighting other areas where the Christian faith has been misinterpreted and corrupted.

In attempting to understand this passage better, the questions were extremely useful, and the text taught the groups much about Jesus' understanding of religion.

1   Why does the entry into Jerusalem described in v.15 differ so markedly from that in v.1-11?
2   What impression does the reader gain about the Temple?
3   What 'sort' of religion would be practised in a Temple like this one?
4   In what ways does the life and 'religion' prescribed by Jesus differ?
5   What does the attitude of the Scribes and Pharisees tell us about the probable reasons for Jesus' crucifixion?
6   In what ways has our 'religion' become like that practised in the Temple and how are we to counteract this?

Notes on the text

It is important to view the cleansing of the Temple in its correct context within the framework of Mark's gospel. The cleansing takes place after Jesus has triumphantly entered into Jerusalem. Mark has shown how Jesus was acclaimed by the people of Jerusalem, but that the glory of this moment cannot detract from the important mission which Jesus has yet to complete.

In cleansing the Temple, Jesus challenges Judaism at its very heart. The Temple was a focal point for pilgrimages as well as worship for the Jews of Jerusalem. Taxes were collected by the Temple and it served as the base for a flourishing economy. (For further discussion on the Temple, see pp. 13 above on 'The First Horizon, Palestine'.)

The slopes of the Mount of Olives were considered part of the Temple precincts, and on the slopes one could find markets selling the animals necessary for sacrifice. The Sanhedrin supervised the running of these markets.

Evidence suggests that there was no trade within the Temple until 30 CE, when it was instituted by Caiaphas. Many were shocked at this proposal to allow a market to operate in the Court of the Gentiles. Access to the interior of the Temple was through the Court of the Gentiles, but certain rules protected it from being reduced to a thoroughfare. This area was not regarded as being significantly sacred.

The moneychangers found employ in the Temple because pilgrims came to Jerusalem from many places with different currencies. Temple dues were paid in the Tyrian coinage because it was closest to the Hebrew shekel. The moneychangers charged a surcharge of 1/24 of a shekel for the exchange.

Doves were sacrificed for a number of reasons: by the poor, by women for purification and by lepers for cleansing. Other larger animals were also sold for sacrificial purposes. Wine, oil, salt and perfumes were also sold in the Court of the Gentiles, serving to turn the area into a market place, especially before feast periods.

Jesus specifically states that he has not only come to the Jews, but to the Gentiles as well, and the defilement of the Gentile area was a source of anger for Jesus. Jesus' anger shows his concern for the sanctity of the Temple as a place of worship. Jesus' response was in line with the command of the Old Testament (Zech.14.21) where traders were barred from trading in the Temple. Jesus shows that the time has been fulfilled and that righteous Gentiles were now gathering in the Temple to worship God (Zech.14.16).

When Jesus quotes from Isaiah (56.7) he shows how the Temple has been defiled and is no longer a house of prayer, but is now a financial concern. It is important to note that Jesus stresses that the Temple is not only for the use of the Jews, but rather for 'all nations'. The presence of the markets in the Court of the Gentiles implied that it had become impossible for the Gentiles to worship God in the Temple.

Jesus again quotes from the Old Testament (Jer.7.11) when he calls the Temple a 'house of robbers'. This understanding of the Temple is in sharp contrast to the image of the Temple as a house of prayer. When Jesus says 'You have made it . . .' he is certainly laying the blame at the door of the Temple authorities.

Jesus' response would not have been missed by Mark's audience in Rome. Apart from attempting to purify a religion which has turned from prayer and worship to financial enterprise, Jesus is stating the right of the Gentiles to participate fully in worshipping at the Temple. He shows how the Gentiles have been excluded from the possibility of worship because of the working of the market, and that they have a right to partake in the Jewish religion and Temple.

Jesus' anger is directed at the priestly authorities for allowing the defilement of the Temple area. It is his anger and accusations which finally make the priestly authorities decide to have him arrested. In strong contrast to the reaction of the priests and scribes is that of the crowds, who are simply amazed at the authority of Jesus' actions. An authoritative act was referred to as a 'new teaching'.

Jesus' concern for the Gentiles and for a true form of worship ultimately brought him nearer to his arrest and death. Obviously, Jesus understood religion in a completely different way to the scribes and priests, and it is Jesus' perception of religion which should serve as a yardstick for Christians today.

Reflections on the text

A careful study of this passage reveals much to Christians of today about how to worship and live the Christian life. The Temple and its financial works set a bad example to non-Jews. The religion was full of empty ritual, and for the Gentiles to worship in a market would have become meaningless. Christians need to examine how their religion is perceived by others. Is Christianity full of meaningless ritual, with people going through the motions merely because they have become traditional?

As we mentioned, this study was done in November, as Christians began thinking about Christmas. Each group felt that the Christmas tradition was similar to the market atmosphere that Jesus was protesting about.

The Christmas period is frequently referred to as 'the festive season'. Christmas has ensured a huge financial trade for those in the retailing and selling areas. The figure of 'Father Christmas' and not the infant Jesus has become synonymous with Christmas. Certainly, for many Christians, Christmas is a meaningful celebration of Jesus' birth, but this time of reflection and worship has largely become defiled.

Seeing Jesus' reaction to the merchants and others in the Temple made us ask what his response to the Christmas celebrations would be. Society has taken the Christ out of Christmas. Just as many people travelled to Jerusalem only for the festivals, so too do many go to church only at Christmas. Church attendance then becomes a matter of tradition rather than an act of worship.

A further spin-off of this defilement of a holy day is the fact that the Christian faith is thrown into disrepute. Many people see Christmas as a meaningless tradition and assume that, in the same way, the Christian religion is meaningless tradition ritual. Obviously, this understanding is not true, but one can certainly see why it came about.

It is clearly the duty of all Christians to react against the commercialism of this holy day. Christmas should be seen by the world as being a meaningful celebration of the birth of Jesus and not as a massive commercial enterprise.

Christmas is not the only example of Christianity becoming an empty religious tradition. Easter is no longer a reflection of Jesus' passion, but has become synonymous with eggs and 'easter bunnies'. Easter greatly increases the trade and turnover of shops, but the important event which it commemorates has become lost amongst the commercial clap-trap. How would Jesus respond to this?

Christians are called to celebrate Christmas and Easter as holy days, days of worship, prayer and praise, and it is their duty to share this understanding with all.

It might be the tinsel and parties of Christmas that is keeping people from Christianity, just as the market distanced the Gentiles from worship. Christians are called to be sensitive to all and must ensure that these holy days are respected in the proper fashion.

A Scholarly Note

This book has been designed for use by the lay-person, but sound academic research lies behind it.

In chapter 2, in discussing the three horizons, a sociological approach has been used. This methodology has been implicit rather than explicit, and was selected because it demonstrates the different aspects of the societies in a clear, easily understandable manner.

In describing Palestine, Freyne* was used extensively. The works of Echegaray, Metzger and Jeremias were also useful in highlighting aspects of Palestinian society. Instead of tracing the history and political developments of Palestine, emphasis has been placed on the socio-economic factors as these are perceived to be more important to the nature and character of the 'Jesus movement'.

Work on the Christian community in Rome was based upon Clevenot. Although it is not accepted by all scholars that Rome was the destination of the second gospel, we believe that the evidence available points to the Christians in Rome as being the recipients of the gospel. The alternative place of composition, namely in or near Galilee, is supported by scholars like Marxsen and Scroggs, but we regarded Clevenot as correct and have thus taken Rome to be the destination.

There has been no discussion of the important issue of the development of the Christian movement from the time of Jesus, when it was based in the rural areas, to the more urban form of Christianity evident in Paul's writings. This development has been noted, but any discussion of the reasons for the change were seen to be outside the scope of this work. The works of Kee, Theissen and Hengel have been consulted to gain an overall understanding of the factors influencing the change, as well as the forms that this change took.

Other issues such as the priority of Mark and the extent of the Messianic secret have not been covered either, but these issues are seldom debated by current scholars and are largely outside the scope of this work.

While many other works on Palestine, Rome and the gospel of Mark were consulted, those contained in the bibliography were the most formative in the earlier sections of this book.

* See 'Some Suggested Readings' for this and other references.

Some Suggested Readings

In working on this study, in addition to the input from the various study groups, numerous works were consulted. The following books were used extensively and would be useful for those interested in reading more about Palestine, Rome or the gospel of Mark.

Belo, F., *A Materialist Reading of the Gospel of Mark*, Orbis Books, (Maryknoll, 1974)

Clevenot, M., *Materialist Approaches to the Bible*, Orbis Books, (Maryknoll, 1985)

Echegaray, H., *The Practice of Jesus*, Orbis Books, (Maryknoll, 1980)

Freyne, S., *Galilee from Alexander the Great to Hadrian: 323 BCE — 135 CE*, Michael Glazier Inc., (Delaware, 1980)

Geza, A., *The Social History of Rome*, Croom Helm, (London, 1975)

Hunter, A.M., *Saint Mark*, SCM Press Ltd, (London, 1978)

Jeremias, J., *Jerusalem in the Time of Jesus*, Fortress Press, (Philadelphia, 1969)

Kee, H.C., *Community of the New Age*, Westminster Press, (Philadelphia, 1977)

Martin, R., *Mark, Evangelist and Theologian*, Zondervan Pub. House, (Michigan, 1972)

Marxsen, W., *The Resurrection of Jesus of Nazareth*, SCM Press Ltd, (London, 1970)

Metzger, B., *The New Testament; Its Background, Growth and Content*, Abingdon Press, (Tennessee, 1965)

Robinson, J.M., *The Problem of History in Mark*, SCM Press Ltd, (London, 1971)

Scroggs, R., The Earliest Hellenistic Christianity, in *Religion in Antiquity: Essays in Memory of E.R. Goodenough*, Ed. J. Neusner, Brill, (Leiden, 1975)

Theissen, G., *The First Followers of Jesus: A Sociological Annalysis of Earliest Christianity*, SCM Press Ltd, (London, 1982)

Commentaries
Anderson, H., *The Gospel of Mark*, Oliphants, (London, 1976)

Lane, W.C., *Commentary on the Gospel of Mark*, W.B. Eerdmans Pub. Co., (Michigan, 1974)

Taylor, V., *The Gospel According to Saint Mark*, McMillan & Co. Ltd, (New York, 1957)